The *Christmas*
You've Always *Longed* For

Personalizing Your Holiday Experience

Written By
David and Karen Mains
Doug and Melissa Timberlake
Nancy S. Gruben

DEVOTIONAL JOURNAL

The Christmas You've Always Longed For
Personalizing Your Holiday Experience

DEVOTIONAL JOURNAL

Written By

David and Karen Mains
Doug and Melissa Timberlake
Nancy S. Gruben

Copyright © 2006 by Mainstay Ministries

Cover Illustration

Steve Creitz

Printed in the United States of America

Contents

Introduction

Christmas always evokes feelings of longing. Almost despite ourselves we begin to expect remarkable things to happen during this season. We yearn for:

- the gathering of family where all are happy to be together.
- time to connect with our circle of friends in meaningful ways.
- the ability to create celebrations that make room for joy and deep feelings.
- ways to create beauty with food, lights, and decorations.
- armistices where hostilities are discarded for interludes of peace.
- the observance of traditions that enrich us.
- the giving and receiving of gifts as true symbols of love and kindness.
- entering into the deep mystery of spiritual truth through the birth of Christ—God taking on human form.

Unfortunately, we are all too often disappointed. Fatigue gives way to crankiness. Stress triggers colds, headaches and influenza. Our holy hopes are diminished by overindulgence and consumerism. Feelings of depression grab at us: Why have we never had enough love or time or energy to do what we wanted to do? Comparisons nag: How come they always have unlimited resources?

The reality of Christmas for many is the family never gathers without fighting, parties with friends are superficial, and some people are constantly lonely. Others are reminded of what they want or need and do not have. Grief can be overwhelming.

Be encouraged! Christmas doesn't have to be this way. Christmas can become what you've always longed for. It can be a positive, holy observance, no matter what your circumstances.

This Seasonal Devotional Journal is designed to help you slow down, choose the most important focus, follow through on your good intents, then really celebrate.

To do all this, we will lead you through the four Sundays of Advent and on to Christmas Day. We believe you will find this devotional journal a remarkable tool that will help you discover practical ways to make this the Christmas you've always longed for.

What Exactly Is Advent?

The word advent means "coming." The season of Advent prepares us to welcome the birth of Christ on Christmas Eve and Christmas Day. Several other facts will help you understand this period of time:

- Advent is observed by millions of Christians throughout the world.
- In liturgical settings, Advent is actually the beginning of the church year.
- Advent always begins four Sundays before Christmas Day.
- Most people who observe Advent do so with some kind of candle-lighting ceremony and the reading of scriptures.

Observing Advent, year after year, not only prepares people to meaningfully celebrate Christ's first coming, the holy festival of Christmas, but it points us toward Christ's second coming as a way of renewing our anticipation of that great day.

Advent, when observed correctly, can help us develop the habit of recognizing the coming of Christ into our everyday lives all the rest of the year.

Research into the traditions of Advent will reveal a wide variety of approaches. We have intentionally designed this devotional journal to lead you through the Advent season and up to December 25, in order to help you create the Christmas you've always longed for.

Following Mary Through The First Christmas

During this Advent Celebration, you'll focus on seeing the Christmas story from Mary's point of view. Mary was an ordinary young woman with an extraordinary trust in God. She was given the exceptional assignment of bringing the Christ child into the world, but still she shared our full human capacity for doubt, discouragement, and fear. It's no wonder that through the ages men and women of God have stood in awe and admiration of her incredible grace and deep faith.

Mary's spiritual and physical path through that very first Christmas is one worthy of our examination. Never again will a human being be given the unique task of carrying and giving birth to the Son of God. But God continues to place and nurture other kinds of seeds in the hearts and minds of his true followers: hopes for genuine change, expectations of a better future, and dreams of meaningful ministry on his behalf.

Wanting to observe and truly celebrate Christmas in a God-honoring fashion is another worthy desire in the hearts of many Christians today. If you are among them, this devotional journal is designed especially for you—to help you pattern these weeks of "waiting with expectation" after Mary's own biblical example.

Following Mary's model of faith, you'll begin to realize the Christmas you've always longed for. More than that, with God's help you'll learn how to wait, watch, and participate as the Lord unfolds and grows other miracles in your life. It's the best process we know for allowing God to meet the true longings of your heart.

How To Use This Devotional Journal
(On Your Own or with Your Church)

If you want to prepare yourself or your entire family for a more meaningful Christmas celebration, this is just the tool you've been looking for! In a fun and easy way this devotional journal will take you through the entire Advent season. Everything you need is right in your hands.

Each day you'll find a scripture, a suggested prayer, a place to journal your thoughts, and an inspirational reading related to the theme "The Christmas You've Always Longed For." Even better, you'll find practical suggestions and how-to ideas for turning your "good intentions" of having a God-honoring Christmas, into reality in your day-to-day life. And there are suggestions for families as well as individuals. You may want to read both the family and individual suggestions to get some extra ideas. But don't think you have to do all the suggestions. That's just what they are—suggestions. Try to do some of them.

Each year, Advent begins four Sundays before Christmas. But the actual dates vary from year to year. That's why this devotional journal has days of the week, not dates, on the top of each page.

If you're having trouble figuring out the dates for the four Advent Sundays this year, get a calendar and count back four Sundays from Christmas (if Christmas is on a Sunday, count back the four Sundays before then). If it would help you, feel free to pencil in the dates on the top of each page.

Each week of Advent, this devotional journal will help you focus on a different aspect of the Christmas you've always longed for. There are five different themes (one for each week of Advent plus one for Christmas Day).

Advent Week 1 .... Slow Down for Reflection

Advent Week 2 .... Keep a Christ-Centered Focus

Advent Week 3 .... Manage the Inevitable Distractions

Advent Week 4 .... Celebrate Whatever Your Circumstances

Christmas Day .... Enjoy a God-pleasing Christmas

As you move along toward Christmas, this devotional journal will help you evaluate, make choices, and carry through on a plan to make this Christmas the best ever—a Christmas that satisfies your true longings for the season. If you're in a church that's using "The Christmas You've Always Longed For" Advent Series, this devotional journal will help prepare you for your weekly worship time as well.

Each day you are reminded of the theme for the week. This is followed by a short scripture related to the sermon from the previous Sunday. Next is a place for you to briefly journal your thoughts. Use this space to record how you are doing as you seek to make this "The Christmas You've Always Longed For". Next is a prayer for the day, again reminding you of the theme for the week. Finally, you will notice a short thought to ponder.

Each Sunday, in place of the practical suggestions, you'll find questions for discussion over a Sunday meal. Talk about them with your spouse or a roommate. (If you live alone, talk them through with a friend or prayer partner.) Or use the questions with your entire family; they're appropriate for all ages. These questions will help you evaluate and plan what's important to you in celebrating a meaningful Christmas.

Also each week, following the Sunday pages, you'll find a simple ceremony that can be used for lighting the candles on a home Advent wreath. See pages 9-11 to learn more about this tradition. There are ceremonies for individuals and couples as well as for families with young children. And there's one for Christmas also. Clear directions for making your own Advent wreath are on pages 10-11. Or you can find a ready-made wreath in a Christian bookstore.

Planning A Home Ceremony

The lighting of an Advent wreath is a part of many Christmas traditions. It's a simple yet meaningful way to officially mark the four Sundays leading up to Christmas. For children, it's a good way to visualize the "countdown" to Christmas Day while keeping in mind the true meaning of the season.

Most Advent wreaths are made using a circle of greenery with four candles. These candles are lighted progressively on each Sunday of Advent. You can light a different candle each week. Or, you might choose to light one candle the first Sunday, two the second, and so on. Nearby, or in the center of the wreath itself, many people place a Christmas candle or Christ candle. This is lit on Christmas Eve or Christmas Day.

Some churches place special significance on the colors of each candle. For your home ceremony you can choose any color candles you wish, although the Christ candle is most often white. Some people also relate each candle to a Christmas symbol (light, hope, joy, peace) or to people in the Christmas story (prophet, angel, shepherd, Magi). Again, this is up to you.

The home ceremonies you'll find in this devotional journal will help you focus on honoring Christ this Christmas season. One ceremony is for individuals and couples and another for families with young children. Use them as they are written, or feel free to adapt them to your own needs.

There are directions for making a simple Advent wreath easily and inexpensively at home on pages 10-11.

The home ceremonies are found on the following pages:

Making An Advent Wreath

Making an Advent wreath is a wonderful project for families or individuals. Children especially love ceremony and tradition and are usually enthusiastic participants. As always, supervise children carefully during the candle lighting and never leave them alone in a room where candles are lit. (A permanent Advent wreath can be bought at your local Christian bookstore.)

Materials:

- Foam wreath form or 12" cardboard circle with 6" hole cut out of the center
- Four candles, 8" or taller (if using cardboard, place the candles in small holders)
- Larger white candle
- Aluminum foil
- Real or artificial greenery, Christmas flowers, and so on
- Hot-glue gun

Directions: Foam Wreath

- Lay the wreath flat on a table and push the candles into the top in an evenly spaced order.
- Remove the candle and line the candle holes with aluminum foil.
- Push short pieces of greenery (real or artificial) into the foam wreath. Cover your wreath completely, keeping the pieces short in order to prevent them from catching fire from the lighted candles.
- Put hot glue on the ends of the candles and press them back into their holes.
- Set the white Christ candle nearby or in the center of the ring in a holder, saucer, or on a pad of foil.

(See illustration on p. 11.)

Directions: Cardboard Circle Wreath

- Mark the four places where your candle holders will stand.
- Use artificial greenery or flowers, gluing them in place on the cardboard and leaving space for the candle holders. Cover your wreath completely, keeping the pieces short in order to prevent them from catching fire from the lighted candles.
- Set the candle holders in place. For added stability, you may wish to tape or glue the holders to the cardboard.
- Set the white Christ candle nearby or in the center of the ring in a holder, saucer, or on a pad of foil.

TODAY'S SCRIPTURE

"You will be with child and give birth to a son,
and you are to give him the name Jesus" (Luke 1:31).

JOURNAL THOUGHTS

_____

_____

_____

_____

_____

_____

TODAY'S PRAYER

Father, the days ahead may be filled with joy; we know they also have the potential to overwhelm or disappoint. Help us today to slow down and evaluate our actions as we look forward to the celebration of the birth of your Son. Amen.

THOUGHT TO PONDER

Come, thou long expected Jesus,

Born to set thy people free;

From our fears and sins release us,

Let us find our rest in thee.

Israel's strength and consolation,

Hope of all the earth thou art:

Dear desire of every nation,

Joy of every longing heart.

-- Charles Wesley, "Come Thou Long Expected Jesus," stanzas 1-2

DISCUSSION QUESTIONS FOR A SUNDAY MEAL

- Share a happy Christmas memory.
- What did you like best about recent Christmases you've celebrated? What did you like least?
- If you could eliminate an activity or two this Christmas season, what would it be and why?
- Name one single experience or activity that helps make Christmas happy for you.
- What crises seem to occur every year around Christmas? How can they be avoided this year?
- In all of your celebrating, what kinds of gifts can you give to the Lord that will take thought and follow-through?

For Individuals or Couples

This ceremony can be used the first Sunday of Advent by individuals or couples.

The First Candle: Slow Down for Reflection

Candle Lighting: As we light this first candle, we begin the season of Advent. In this moment, we slow our hearts and minds and ready our spirit for the celebration of Christ's birth.

New Testament Scripture: Read Luke 1:26-45

Reflection: Mary, Jesus' mother, must have been confused by the news of Christ's coming birth, wondering what the days ahead would bring. To help sort things out, she traveled to the home of Elizabeth, an older woman who was also having a special child. Here, Mary had a friend with whom she could talk and carefully consider the wonder of the Christmas miracle to come.

Prayer: Father, the days ahead may be filled with joy; we know they also have the potential to be over-whelming or disappointing. As we prepare to celebrate Christmas, help us to slow down. Help us to evaluate what we really want and need during the weeks ahead. Remind us daily that only you can truly satisfy the longings of our hearts – during this special season and throughout the year. Amen.

Old Testament Scripture: Read Isaiah 7:14

Sing: Sing a favorite hymn or Christmas carol.

For Families With Young Children

This ceremony can be used the first Sunday of Advent by families with young children.

The First Candle: Slow Down for Reflection

Parent: Today we light the first candle in our Advent wreath.

Children: Christmas is coming!

Parent: I wonder what the days ahead will be like. Will we be busy and rushed? Or will we take time to slow down and think about what's really important?

Children: Christmas is coming!

Parent: That's what the angel told Mary. He told her, "Jesus is going to be born. You will be his mother." Mary knew the days ahead might be hard. That's why she took time to visit her cousin Elizabeth. Together they talked about God and what was coming in the days ahead.

Children: Christmas is coming!

Parent: As we light this first candle in our Advent wreath, we promise to slow down, too. We promise to think and talk together about what's really important at Christmas time. *[Light the first candle]*

All together: Christmas is coming!

MONDAY
Advent Week 1

TODAY'S SCRIPTURE

"He [Jesus] will be great and will be called the Son of the Most High. The Lord God will give him the throne of his father David, and he will reign over the house of Jacob forever; his kingdom will never end." (Luke 1:32-33)

JOURNAL THOUGHTS

_____

_____

_____

_____

_____

_____

_____

_____

_____

_____

_____

TODAY'S PRAYER

Jesus, you are Lord of your kingdom. Reign over our lives in this busy season and help us slow down to reflect on those things that are lasting. Amen.

THOUGHT TO PONDER

Corrie ten Boom asked, "Is prayer your steering wheel or your spare tire?" This Christmas, make prayer your steering wheel. Let God guide you through the season. Don't save your prayers for the crises that may arise. Use prayers extravagantly, generously every day.

PRACTICAL SUGGESTIONS

For Families: Adopt a Family Motto

Consider adopting a family motto for the Christmas season this year. Choose a motto that helps alleviate some of the extra stress and unrealistic expectations. For example, this motto might relate to decorating, shopping, and baking: "If it's more burden than fun, don't do it!" Or, for activities around the home, "Jesus would rather see beautiful hearts than beautiful decorations."

For Individuals: Send Cards in January

If the thought of addressing dozens of Christmas cards is already producing stress, consider sending them in January instead. It will be a nice surprise for friends and family, and they'll be more likely to have a chance to sit down and really enjoy reading what you've written. It's also a good opportunity to respond specifically to the cards and letters you receive in December, letting friends know you've read their notes with care.

TUESDAY
Advent Week 1

TODAY'S SCRIPTURE

"How will this be," Mary asked the angel, since I am a virgin?" The angel answered, "The Holy Spirit will come upon you, and the power of the Most High will overshadow you. So the holy one to be born will be called the Son of God." (Luke 1:34-35)

JOURNAL THOUGHTS

_____

_____

_____

_____

_____

_____

_____

_____

TODAY'S PRAYER

Son of God, help us take time to reflect on how we might truly worship you, the Holy One, this Christmas. Amen.

THOUGHT TO PONDER

O come, Thou Dayspring, come and cheer

Our spirits by Thine advent here;

Disperse the gloomy clouds of night,

And death's dark shadows put to flight.

Rejoice! Rejoice!

Emmanuel Shall come to thee, O Israel!

-- *9th century Latin hymn, "O Come, O Come, Emmanuel," stanza 2*

PRACTICAL SUGGESTIONS

For Families: Make a Baby Cradle Reminder

Dig through your attic or storage space for an old baby cradle, decorate it, and then place it in a busy area of your house. Use this as a symbol of what the Christmas season is really about. Let the cradle be a constant reminder to slow down and truly focus on the coming birth of the Christ child. You could place wrapped gifts or even baby items inside or around the cradle. (After Christmas you might give these baby items to a newborn or donate them to a crisis pregnancy center.)

For Individuals: Catch a Sunrise

Make it a point to wake up one morning to watch a sunrise. Use this time of quiet reflection to evaluate your Christmas preparations. Make sure you're not getting caught up in the unhealthy patterns that seem to trap you from year to year. Focus on the fact that Jesus is the Light of the World. Ask him to show you how to make the days ahead as joyful and Christ-centered as they can be.

WEDNESDAY
Advent Week 1

TODAY'S SCRIPTURE

"Even Elizabeth your relative is going to have a child in her old age, and she who was said to be barren is in her sixth month. For nothing is impossible with God."

"I am the Lord's servant," Mary answered. "May it be to me as you have said."
Then the angel left her. (Luke 1:36-38)

JOURNAL THOUGHTS

_____

_____

_____

_____

_____

_____

_____

_____

TODAY'S PRAYER

Lord, let each of us slow down long enough to say, "May it be to me as you have said," knowing you want the best for us this Christmas season. We feel privileged to be your servants. Amen.

THOUGHT TO PONDER

God grant you the light in Christmas, which is faith;

the warmth of Christmas, which is love;

the belief in Christmas, which is truth;

the all of Christmas, which is Christ.

-- Wilda English

PRACTICAL SUGGESTIONS

For Families: Celebrate Past Holiday Memories

Thank the Lord for the happy Christmas memories you have as a family. Take time out together to watch old super-eight movies and videos of former family gatherings or to look through family photo albums. Enjoy the memories these pictures evoke. Laugh at the outdated clothing styles, remember and tell stories about relatives and friends, and talk about the places you used to live. Evaluate what was special about those times, and make sure to incorporate those elements into this year's celebration.

For Individuals: Consider the Holiday "Too Much's"

Examine the holiday "too much's" in your life. Do you spend too much, do too much, expect too much, consume too much, and want too much? Ask yourself: What are the most important values for me this season? Then, before letting the "too much's" run away with you, plan how you can focus first on the values you cherish.

A "too much" I want to avoid this year is _____

Thursday
Advent Week 1

Today's Scripture

At that time Mary got ready and hurried to a town in the hill country of Judea, where she entered Zechariah's home and greeted Elizabeth. (Luke 1:39-40)

Journal Thoughts

_____

_____

_____

_____

_____

_____

_____

_____

_____

_____

Today's Prayer

Father, help us to keep talking with family and friends about this season of miracles. Give us wisdom, perspective, and support to make the most of the days ahead. Amen.

Thought to Ponder

God of God, Light of light,

Lo! He abhors not the Virgin's womb;

Very God, begotten not created:

O come, let us adore him . . . Christ the Lord.

-- *Latin hymn, "O Come, All Ye Faithful," stanza 2*

Practical Suggestions

For Families: Attend a Special Holiday Event

The Christmas season is filled with many free and inspiring events. As a family, plan now to take time to see a community production or a church Nativity play. Or set aside a special evening to enjoy a cantata or town square concert. By providing a break from the busyness, these holiday events can help prepare your heart to celebrate the true meaning of Christmas. Note: This is not to add "busy work," but to help you concentrate on what's important in this season.

A date we would like to reserve as a family is _____

for _____

For Individuals: Use the Gift of Wasted Time

Take "wasted" time as a gift from the Lord, and use it to slow down and focus on him. When you choose the "wrong" line at the grocery store, use the extra minutes to take a deep breath and enjoy a moment of quiet. Instead of tapping impatiently on the microwave while your bagel is defrosting, pray for one of your family members. And if you get caught in traffic, turn down the radio and sing every Christmas carol or praise hymn you can remember.

FRIDAY
Advent Week 1

TODAY'S SCRIPTURE

When Elizabeth heard Mary's greeting, the baby leaped in her womb, and Elizabeth was filled with the Holy Spirit. In a loud voice she exclaimed: "Blessed are you among women, and blessed is the child you will bear! But why am I so favored, that the mother of my Lord should come to me?" (Luke 1:41-43)

JOURNAL THOUGHTS

_____

_____

_____

_____

_____

_____

TODAY'S PRAYER

Lord, help us to slow down for reflection, so that when Christmas arrives, our hearts will exclaim, "Blessed is the Christ child born today!"

THOUGHT TO PONDER

O that birth forever blessed,

When the Virgin, full of grace,

By the Holy Ghost conceiving,

Bore the Savior of our race;

And the Babe, the world's Redeemer,

First revealed his sacred face.

-- Marcus A. Prudentius, "Of the Father's Love Begotten," stanza 2

PRACTICAL SUGGESTIONS

For Families: Exchange Letters

Would you like to simplify people's lives and bless them at the same time? Consider a letter exchange in which family members write out words of appreciation instead of or in addition to purchasing gifts. When you gather to celebrate on Christmas the letters could be exchanged or read aloud. A letter exchange this year could be the solution to a host of economic and energy excesses during the holidays.

For Individuals: Find Your Elizabeth

Follow Mary's example. During a time of confusion in her life, Mary knew the importance of finding a trusted friend who could help her slow down the racing that was going on in her mind. Elizabeth was a wise, older woman. Together they spent time talking through what was happening to Mary. Somehow in the midst of overwhelming circumstances, Mary was able to find peace. What about you? Do you have someone older and wiser in your life who can help sort through the chaotic aspects of Christmas? Ask for advice, pray together, and trust this friend to keep you accountable.

TODAY'S SCRIPTURE

[Elizabeth said to Mary] "As soon as the sound of your greeting reached my ears, the baby in my womb leaped for joy. Blessed is she who has believed that what the Lord has said to her will be accomplished!" (Luke 1:44-45)

JOURNAL THOUGHTS

_____

_____

_____

_____

_____

_____

_____

_____

_____

TODAY'S PRAYER

Lord, help us believe that as we reflect and plan well, we can experience the Christmas we've always longed for. Amen.

THOUGHT TO PONDER

Joy to the world!

The Lord is come:

Let earth receive her King;

Let every heart prepare him room,

And heaven and nature sing.

-- Isaac Watts, "Joy to the World!" stanza 1

PRACTICAL SUGGESTIONS

For Families: Give Wise Men Gifts

Gift-giving should never be all-consuming. Consider simplifying things this year by giving each child only three gifts—representing the gold, frankincense, and myrrh the wise men brought Jesus. Consider giving gifts with different purposes, such as one to read, one to wear, and one gift to enjoy with others.

For Individuals: Take a Trip

Mary took a trip to the hill country of Judea in order to find a place where she could slow down and work through what was happening. Figure out what the equivalent of Mary's trip might be in your situation. Maybe it's you and your spouse or a special friend going out for coffee to talk about what's important to you this Christmas. Or maybe you need a full family meeting around a big bowl of popcorn. Talk about how well you honored Christ last Christmas season and whether you need to change anything this year.

TODAY'S SCRIPTURE

And Mary said: "My soul glorifies the Lord and my spirit rejoices in God my Savior, for he has been mindful of the humble state of his servant. From now on all generations will call me blessed, for the Mighty One has done great things for me—holy is his name." (Luke 1:46-49)

JOURNAL THOUGHTS

_____

_____

_____

_____

_____

TODAY'S PRAYER

Mighty God, you have done great things for us. As we prepare to celebrate the birth of our Savior, help us to focus on what is truly honoring to your Son. Amen.

THOUGHT TO PONDER

Isaiah 'twas foretold it,

The Rose I have in mind,

With Mary we behold it,

The Virgin Mother kind.

To show God's love aright,

She bore to us a Savior,

When half spent was the night.

-- *15th century German carol, "Lo! How a Rose E'er Blooming." stanza 2*

DISCUSSION QUESTIONS FOR A SUNDAY MEAL

- If Jesus were coming to your house, what special touch might you add to make certain he would feel welcome?
- If Jesus sat down at the table with you, what might you change in your conversation?
- Whom would Jesus want you to tell about his birthday this Christmas?
- Which of your Christmas activities would make Jesus especially happy?
- How can you plan now to make sure you have time to attend church services this Christmas as a way of honoring Jesus through your worship?

For Individuals or Couples

This ceremony can be used the second Sunday of Advent by individuals or couples.

The Second Candle: Keep a Christ-Centered Focus

Candle Lighting: Today as we light this second Advent candle, help us to focus on what is most important. Let this candle symbolize the praise we will offer to God during this Christmas season.

New Testament Scripture: Read Luke 1:46-55

Reflection: Mary sang, "My soul glorifies the Lord and my spirit rejoices in God my Savior" (Luke 1:46-47). During these days before Christ's birth, Mary focused on what was most important and most honoring to the Lord. Mary took time to praise God.

Prayer: Father, we long for a deep and meaningful Christmas—something more than activities can provide. Because the most joyous celebrations honor a person or an event, this Christmas we want to honor Jesus and the miracle of his birth. Help us today to focus on the things that are truly honoring to your Son. Remind us that this is the best way to experience the miracle of Christmas. Amen

Old Testament Scripture: Read Isaiah 42:1-9

Sing: Sing a favorite hymn or Christmas carol.

For Families With Young Children
This ceremony can be used the second Sunday of Advent by families with young children.

The Second Candle: Keep a Christ-Centered Focus

Parent: Today we light the second candle in our Advent wreath.

Children: Christmas is coming!

Parent: As we light this candle, let's think about the very first Christmas. What was important?

Children: Christmas is coming!

Parent: When Mary, Jesus mother, knew Christmas was coming, she didn't go to any parties. Mary didn't even decorate a tree. She took time to sing and praise God. And God was happy with her.

Children: Christmas is coming!

Parent: As we light this second candle in our Advent wreath, we promise to focus on what makes God happy at Christmas. He is happy when we sing and praise and honor him. That's the very best way we can be a part of God's Christmas miracle.
[Light the second candle]

All together: Christmas is coming!
(You may wish to conclude your ceremony with a praise chorus or Christmas carol)

Monday
Advent Week 2

Today's Scripture

"[God's] mercy extends to those who fear him, from generation to generation. He has performed mighty deeds with his arm; he has scattered those who are proud in their inmost thoughts." (Luke 1:50-51)

Journal Thoughts

_____

_____

_____

_____

_____

_____

Today's Prayer

Lord, this season help us keep a Christ-centered focus so that the true meaning of Christmas might be remembered from generation to generation. Amen.

Thought to Ponder

Good Christian men, rejoice,
With heart, and soul, and voice;
Now ye hear of endless bliss:
Jesus Christ was born for this!
He hath oped the heav'nly door,
And man is blessed evermore.
Christ was born for this!
Christ was born for this!
-- John Mason Neale, "Good Christian Men, Rejoice," stanza 2

PRACTICAL SUGGESTIONS

For Families: Tell Holiday Stories

As you plan times for your family (or extended family) to be together, set aside a time for scriptural story-telling. The upcoming home ceremonies may be a good time to plan this. Pick a passage and then design creative ways to read it aloud. If you have young children, let them act out the narrative. Help them decide how to dramatically interpret the familiar passage. Feel free to use props and costumes to enhance the storytelling time. Don't be afraid to have fun! The Christmas message is, at its heart, a message of joy.

For Individuals: Give a Christmas Pardon

As Christmas approaches, state governors often grant a pardon to certain prisoners as a special act of clemency. Maybe you could best honor your Lord this Christmas by also giving a Christmas pardon to someone you've locked out of your life. Who is someone who needs your forgiveness? Write on a piece of paper that person's offense and what you feel is owed you. Then write out, "I, (your name), grant clemency to (his or her name) on (date)." Begin to live in accordance with your declaration and enjoy the new freedom forgiveness can bring.

Tuesday
Advent Week 2

Today's Scripture

"[God] has brought down rulers from their thrones but has lifted up the humble. He has filled the hungry with good things but has sent the rich away empty." (Luke 1:52-53)

Journal Thoughts

_____

_____

_____

_____

_____

_____

_____

_____

_____

_____

_____

Today's Prayer

Father, as we focus this Christmas on what is truly honoring to your Son, let us remember your love for the humble and needy. Amen.

Thought to Ponder

The most vivid memories of Christmases past are usually not of gifts given or received, but of the spirit of love, the special warmth of Christmas worship, the cherished little habits of the home.

-- *Lois Rand*

Practical Suggestions

For Families: Gather Your Swaddling Clothes

Help your children sort through their closets and gather clothes they haven't worn this year and probably won't wear again. Place them in a festive bag and donate them to a homeless shelter or the Salvation Army. Think of them as garments given in the name of Christ.

For Individuals: Serve Others with Joy

Local hospitals, convalescent homes, homeless shelters, soup kitchens, and jails can many times use volunteers during the Christmas season. When serving others, do so as though you were serving Christ. This could be the most powerful gift you give! Serving with the spirit of joy can be a special way you show the Christ child honor this season. Note: Sometimes volunteers are plentiful in December, and organizations don't need any more people. If this is the case, consider volunteering in January or February when the need is greater.

WEDNESDAY
Advent Week 2

TODAY'S SCRIPTURE

"[God] has helped his servant Israel, remembering to be merciful to Abraham and his descendants forever, even as he said to our fathers." (Luke 1:54-55)

JOURNAL THOUGHTS

_____

_____

_____

_____

_____

_____

_____

_____

TODAY'S PRAYER

Father, help us today to focus on the things that are truly honoring to your Son. Remind me that this is the best way to experience the true miracle of Christmas. Amen.

THOUGHT TO PONDER

Heaven's arches rang when the angels sang,

Proclaiming Thy royal decree,

But in lowly birth didst Thou come to earth

And in great humility.

O come to my heart, Lord Jesus:

There is room in my heart for Thee!

-- *Emily E. S. Elliott, "Thou Didst Leave Thy Throne," stanza 2*

Practical Suggestions

For Families: Remember Those Who Are Alone

Make a decision to invite someone who will be alone at Christmas to join you for one evening of your Christmas celebration. Reach out to a widow, international student, or someone who has recently been divorced. Welcome strangers, the weary, the less fortunate, the hungry. Help them celebrate by giving them the gift of friendship and love.

For Individuals: Mark Your Calendar

Make sure to schedule a Christmas Eve or Christmas Day church service into your holiday planning. Find out right now which ones are available, and make that given time a priority in your schedule. Once it's on the calendar, that will help you plan other holiday gatherings around your time in the Lord's house. Going to church for a holiday service is an appropriate way to honor Christ.

THURSDAY
Advent Week 2

TODAY'S SCRIPTURE

When it was time for Elizabeth to have her baby, she gave birth to a son. Her neighbors and relatives heard that the Lord had shown her great mercy, and they shared her joy. (Luke 1:57-58)

JOURNAL THOUGHTS

TODAY'S PRAYER

Lord, help us to keep a Christ-centered focus this season so that we can share in the joy of the first Christmas. Amen.

THOUGHT TO PONDER

Joy is for all men. It does not depend on circumstance or condition: if it did, it could only be for the few ... it is the wealth of the soul's whole being when it is filled with the spirit of Jesus, which is the spirit of eternal love.
-- *Horace Bushnell, quoted in M. V. Nelson's An Anthology of Joy*

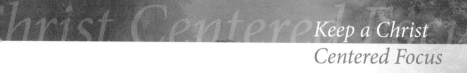
Practical Suggestions

For Families: Hide Scripture Verses

Hide Scripture verses about Christ's coming underneath your children's pillows to read before bedtime or under their cereal bowls to read at the beginning of the day. Use these as a way to build excitement and expectation each day until Christmas. You could use passages from Luke 1 and 2, or Isaiah 9.

For Individuals: Give Gifts with Spiritual Significance

Are you struggling with gift ideas for certain people? Christmas is the ideal time to share your faith with neighbors, acquaintances, coworkers, and family members—both Christian and non-Christian. Consider honoring Christ this Christmas by giving gifts that help others focus on the true meaning of the season. Give a contemporary study Bible or a tape of worshipful Christmas carols. Find a beautifully illustrated Christmas storybook for children or include a printed Nativity meditation with your gifts of holiday baking. You'll likely find that those receiving these pieces will be deeply appreciative and will know that they speak of faith in Christ.

FRIDAY
Advent Week 2

TODAY'S SCRIPTURE

On the eighth day they came to circumcise the child, and they were going to name him after his father Zechariah, but his mother spoke up and said, "No! He is to be called John." (Luke 1:59-60)

JOURNAL THOUGHTS

_____
_____
_____
_____
_____
_____
_____
_____
_____
_____

TODAY'S PRAYER

Father, as John was to prepare the way for the Messiah, let our focus be on preparing to truly honor Christ this Christmas. Amen.

THOUGHT TO PONDER

Every Christian needs a half hour of prayer each day, except when he is busy, then he needs an hour.

-- *St. Francis de Sales*

PRACTICAL SUGGESTIONS

For Families: Make a Gift of Time

Christ's coming shows us the importance of relationships. Consider giving gifts of time: tickets to a concert, a day spent together in a nearby city, an evening doing a special activity. Purchase a tourist's guide that highlights special events or places for your geographic region. Allow each family member to choose one outing he or she would like to share with you during the coming year.

For Individuals: Write a Letter to Jesus

Explain to Jesus why you're looking forward to his coming birthday. Tell him what his arrival means to you and how he is welcome in your heart and home. Writing things down may help focus your thoughts in a way nothing else does. Save the letter and privately read it aloud to the Lord on Christmas Eve as a way to ensure that this special time of year is the best it can possibly be.

TODAY'S SCRIPTURE

They said to [Elizabeth], "There is no one among your relatives who has that name [John]." Then they made signs to his father [Zechariah], to find out what he would like to name the child. He asked for a writing tablet, and to everyone's astonishment he wrote, "His name is John." Immediately his mouth was opened and his tongue was loosed, and he began to speak, praising God. The neighbors were all filled with awe, and throughout the hill country of Judea people were talking about all these things. Everyone who heard this wondered about it, asking "What then is this child going to be?" For the Lord's hand was with him. (Luke 1:61-66)

JOURNAL THOUGHTS

_____

_____

_____

_____

_____

TODAY'S PRAYER

Lord, let us honor you with our praises as we live out the busy days of Advent. And help us to plan a special time when we can focus on worship this Christmas. Amen.

THOUGHT TO PONDER

On Jordan's bank the Baptist's cry

Announces that the Lord is nigh;

Awake and hearken, For he brings

Glad tidings of the King of kings.

-- *Charles Coffin, "On Jordan's Bank", stanza 1*

PRACTICAL SUGGESTIONS

For Families: Play Christmas Carol Lullabies

If you are musically inclined, consider playing carols on the piano each night after the children are tucked in bed (or listening to a Christmas CD or cassette). This will be a special way for your children to focus their thoughts on Jesus during these weeks of Advent. And how wonderful for them to fall asleep while listening to Christmas music!

For Individuals: Tuck a Song in Your Heart

Choose a song you'll adopt as your own for these days before Christmas. Start to sing it to yourself repeatedly. It could be a standard carol such as "Joy to the world, the Lord is come, let earth receive her king … let every heart prepare him room." Or, perhaps you'd like to commit to memory all the words of a praise hymn or chorus. Say, "I'll make this song my own for this Christmas." Buy a tape or CD of whatever the song is. Tell yourself, "Before another day passes I'll let this music start to envelop me with the wonder of God's Christmas miracle."

TODAY'S SCRIPTURE

In those days Caesar Augustus issued a decree that a census should be taken of the entire Roman world. (This was the first census that took place while Quirinius was governor of Syria.) And everyone went to his own town to register. (Luke 2:1-3)

JOURNAL THOUGHTS

_____

_____

_____

_____

_____

_____

_____

_____

_____

_____

_____

_____

TODAY'S PRAYER

Father, in spite of the complications that arise during these busy days, don't let us get sidetracked. Help us to follow through on the things that are most important. Amen.

THOUGHT TO PONDER

Jesus is God spelling himself out in language that man can understand.

-- S. D. Gordon

Discussion Questions for a Sunday Meal

- What has happened in the last week that is keeping you from remembering that this is Christ's birthday coming?
- What do you need to do today to ensure that you take time to focus on Jesus?
- Can you guess what is the hardest thing about Christmas for the important people in your life?
- Is there anything you should cut out of your schedule in the next two weeks?
- Is there anything important that you haven't made time for yet this Christmas season? How can you be sure to fit this into your schedule?

For Individuals or Couples

This ceremony can be used the third Sunday of Advent by individuals or couples.

The Third Candle: Manage the Inevitable Distractions

Candle Lighting: With the lighting of this third candle in the wreath, the season of Advent is already half complete. Let this candle symbolize our intention to follow through on what is truly important during this Christmas season.

New Testament Scripture: Read Luke 2:1-5

Reflection: This is the time that days grow busier. Forgotten tasks overwhelm us. Mary and Joseph also faced many distractions. During the long journey to Bethlehem, they were probably tired and uncomfortable. Yet they focused on what God wanted them to do and where God wanted them to be.

Prayer: Father, it seems that as Christmas comes closer, the days grow busier. It's so easy to get distracted from what is truly significant. Throughout this special season, help us to continue to honor you in our thoughts and activities. Keep us from becoming sidetracked. Remind us today to follow through on the things we know are most important and most honoring to you. Amen.

Old Testament Scripture: Read Isaiah 9:2-7

Sing: Sing a favorite hymn or Christmas carol.

For Families With Young Children

This ceremony can be used the third Sunday of Advent by families with young children.

The Third Candle: Manage the Inevitable Distractions

Parent: It's time to light the third candle. That means we're more than halfway to Christmas!

Children: Christmas is coming!

Parent: Remember how we promised to focus on what is most important at Christmas? We said we'd work hard to find time to praise and honor God.

Children: Christmas is coming!

Parent: When Mary and Joseph rode the donkey to Bethlehem, that was a hard trip. They had to go over 100 miles. They were tired. But they didn't forget what was most important. They kept thinking about the baby coming from God—the Christmas miracle!

Children: Christmas is coming!

Parent: As we light the third candle, we, too, want to remember what is most important at Christmas. We will keep thinking about Jesus and praising him.
[Light the third candle]

All together: Christmas is coming!

MONDAY
Advent Week 3

TODAY'S SCRIPTURE

So Joseph also went up from the town of Nazareth in Galilee to Judea, to Bethlehem the town of David, because he belonged to the house and line of David. He went there to register with Mary, who was pledged to be married to him and was expecting a child. (Luke 2:4-5)

JOURNAL THOUGHTS

_____

_____

_____

_____

TODAY'S PRAYER

Lord, help us, like Mary and Joseph, to manage the distractions that would keep us from doing what you want us to do this Christmas. Show us what steps we can take to make sure we follow your priorities. Amen.

THOUGHT TO PONDER

O little town of Bethlehem,
How still we see thee lie!
Above thy deep and dreamless sleep
The silent stars go by;
Yet in thy dark streets shineth
The everlasting Light;
The hopes and fears of all the years
Are met in thee tonight.
-- *Phillips Brooks, "O Little Town of Bethlehem," stanza 1*

PRACTICAL SUGGESTIONS

For Families: Establish a Christmas Book Tradition

Make it a tradition to visit a bookstore to buy a Christmas book to read as a family. You'll find a wide selection of beautifully illustrated books for children of all ages. Buy one new book each Christmas. Write a special message for the family inside the book, along with the year it was purchased. Together, view this family story time as an activity that honors the Lord. As your collection builds over the years, get out the whole pile early in December and read, read, read!

For Individuals: Establish a Christmas Music Library

One way to keep focused and prepare your heart and home for Christ's coming is to collect a library of seasonal religious music. Declare a "Christmas moratorium" on television for several hours each evening. In its place, let the melodies and lyrics of sacred music cleanse and prepare your heart for Christmas. Add to your library from year to year.

TUESDAY

Advent Week 3

TODAY'S SCRIPTURE

"But you, Bethlehem Ephrathah, though you are small among the clans of Judah, out of you will come for me one who will be ruler over Israel, whose origins are from old, from ancient times." (Micah 5:2)

JOURNAL THOUGHTS

_____

_____

_____

_____

_____

_____

_____

_____

_____

_____

TODAY'S PRAYER

Father, amidst our daily distractions, thank you for the reminder of your plans "from old." Help us take time to truly appreciate the gift of your Son. Amen.

THOUGHT TO PONDER

Let us not flutter too high, but remain by the manger and the swaddling clothes of Christ, "in whom dwelleth all the fullness of the Godhead bodily." There a man cannot fail of God, but finds him most certainly.

-- *Martin Luther*

Practical Suggestions

For Families: Put Together a Christmas Puzzle

Choose a puzzle that in some way relates to the Nativity story, and spend some time as a family assembling it. You may want to place the puzzle on a special table that is accessible to everyone. Make it your goal to finish by Christmas Day. It could be that your whole family works on the puzzle at one time, or maybe family members could work on it individually as they pass by the table.

For Individuals: Find a Place of Sanctuary

Set aside some time to be quiet. Find a place where you won't be distracted (an empty church sanctuary, a bench in the park, an empty office, etc.) Take this opportunity just to sit and be quiet. Tell God where you are struggling this Christmas season, and ask him to help you keep your focus. Most of all, though, just relax and ponder Christ's coming and the true meaning of this Christmas season.

TODAY'S SCRIPTURE

"*Therefore the Lord himself will give you a sign: The virgin will be with child and will give birth to a son, and will call him Immanuel.*" (Isaiah 7:14)

JOURNAL THOUGHTS

_____

_____

_____

_____

_____

_____

_____

_____

_____

_____

_____

TODAY'S PRAYER

Immanuel, "God with us," walk with us through our crowded days. Give us grace to manage distractions and to concentrate on what's significant. Amen.

THOUGHT TO PONDER

They were all looking for a king

To slay their foes and lift them high:

Thou cam'st a little baby thing

That made a woman cry.

-- *George Macdonald, "That Holy Thing"*

PRACTICAL SUGGESTIONS

For Families: Go Stargazing

Large cities often have planetariums with shows that feature the journey of the wise men. Enjoy these opportunities as a family while they are available. Or simply stand outside with a night sky guide in hand and point out the constellations you haven't noticed for too long. Talk together about the wise men who, in order to worship Jesus, followed through on what they knew was important. (Some scholars say that it was a two-year journey). Let the night stars be a constant reminder for you and your family to follow through like the Magi did, with what you've decided is important this season.

For Individuals: Pray for Your Pastor

Christmas can be a busy and even overwhelming time for pastors. There is so much to plan and so much to do along with the regular church activities. And there can be so many distractions—illness, family obligations, social opportunities. Pray for your pastor. Ask God to provide discernment and strength in this busy time. And pray that God will bless your pastor's family with the Christmas they've always longed for.

THURSDAY
Advent Week 3

TODAY'S SCRIPTURE

Nevertheless, there will be no more gloom for those who were in distress. In the past [God] humbled the land of Zebulun and the land of Naphtali, but in the future he will honor Galilee of the Gentiles, by the way of the sea, along the Jordan—The people walking in darkness have seen a great light; on those living in the land of the shadow of death a light has dawned. (Isaiah 9:1-2)

JOURNAL THOUGHTS

_____

_____

_____

_____

_____

_____

_____

_____

TODAY'S PRAYER

Father, let your light dawn on us today, so that we can manage our distractions and follow through on what's most important this Christmas. Amen.

THOUGHT TO PONDER

Jesus Christ is not the best human being, He is a Being Who cannot be accounted for by the human race at all. He is not man becoming God, but God Incarnate, God coming into human flesh, coming into it from outside. His life is the Highest and the Holiest entering in at the lowliest door.

-- *Oswald Chambers, My Utmost for His Highest, December 25*

PRACTICAL SUGGESTIONS

For Families: Go on a Local Farm Outing

Gather the family together and plan a special trip to a nearby farm. Pause to reflect on the conditions and complications Joseph and Mary had to face when giving birth to their first child. How did they keep focused on what was most important during that time? Also consider the protection, quiet, and shelter the stable provided away from a noisy, crowded inn.

For Individuals: Place Sticky Note Reminders

Perhaps as Christmas draws closer and complications multiply, you need to remind yourself of Christ's coming. Why not write the words "Just a little longer, and the day of his coming will be here!" on sticky notes. Plaster the reminders in full view—at the top of your Christmas lists, on the refrigerator, your bathroom mirror, or somewhere in your day organizer. These reminders will help you view the season with expectation rather than the feeling of dread or fatigue.

FRIDAY
Advent Week 3

TODAY'S SCRIPTURE

In those days and at that time I will make a righteous Branch sprout from David's line; he will do what is just and right in the land. In those days Judah will be saved and Jerusalem will live in safety. This is the name by which it will be called: The Lord Our Righteousness. (Jeremiah 33:15-16)

JOURNAL THOUGHTS

_____

_____

_____

TODAY'S PRAYER

Lord, help us to follow your example by doing what is "just and right" this Christmas. Don't let our distractions keep us from honoring you. Amen.

THOUGHT TO PONDER

The darkest time in the year,

The poorest place in the town,

Cold, and a taste of fear,

Man and woman alone,

What can we hope for here?

More light than we can learn,

More wealth than we can treasure,

More love than we can earn,

More peace than we can measure,

Because one child is born.

-- *Christopher Fry*

PRACTICAL SUGGESTIONS

For Families: Take a Quiet Evening to Ask Good Questions

In the middle of the chaos of the season, sometimes we don't take advantage of the time we do have. Take time to treasure the gift of family. Do you know the answers your children or spouse would give to some of these questions? What was one of the best Christmas gifts you've ever received? A favorite Christmas memory? Most disappointing Christmas? What is your favorite holiday dinner item? What is one thing you're really looking forward to this Christmas?

For Individuals: Sign Up for a Church Nursery Experience

Sign up to volunteer in the church nursery for one time in the near future. While caring for the babies, reflect on how God came to us in the form of a helpless infant. Notice a child's tiny hands, toes, and eyelashes, and think about the innocence and purity of a newborn. Let this experience help you focus on what's important—the meaning of Christ's coming to our world as a little babe.

Saturday
Advent Week 3

Today's Scripture

A shoot will come up from the stump of Jesse; from his roots a Branch will bear fruit. The Spirit of the Lord will rest on him—the Spirit of wisdom and of understanding, the Spirit of counsel and of power, the Spirit of knowledge and of the fear of the Lord. (Isaiah 11:1-2)

Journal Thoughts

_____
_____
_____
_____
_____

Today's Prayer

Lord, please give us your wisdom and understanding to order our increasingly busy days. When distractions arise, keep us focused on what's most important this season. Amen.

Thought to Ponder

Lo, how a Rose e'er blooming

From tender stem hath sprung!

Of Jesse's lineage coming

As seers of old have sung.

It came a blossom bright,

Amid the cold of winter,

When half spent was the night.

-- *15th century German hymn, "Lo, How a Rose E'er Blooming," stanza 1*

PRACTICAL SUGGESTIONS

For Families: Feed the Birds

This is a great time to create a Christmas tree for the birds and squirrels. Children can string popcorn or apple slices, roll pinecones in peanut butter and bird seed, or simply hang net packages of suet available from your local meat department. Talk about the many animals who are mentioned in the Bible and the ones that may have been present at the birth of Christ. Read Jesus' words in Matthew 6:26 that remind us how the heavenly Father feeds the birds and also cares for us.

For Individuals: Celebrate Birth

This year, consider celebrating Christmas by taking a baby gift to a crisis pregnancy center. Spend as much or as little as you like. Gifts may be new or good-as-new. Remember that Christmas is the celebration of birth, a baby's birth. That baby was Jesus who grew to be the Christ, the Savior of the world! While at the center, think about the child who will be receiving your present. He or she may be poor or perhaps even homeless. Remember the similar circumstances Jesus faced when he was born.

TODAY'S SCRIPTURE

While [Mary and Joseph] were there, the time came for the baby to be born, and she gave birth to her firstborn, a son. She wrapped him in cloths and placed him in a manger, because there was no room for them in the inn. (Luke 2:6-7)

JOURNAL THOUGHTS

_____

_____

_____

_____

_____

TODAY'S PRAYER

Father, remind us today that we can celebrate the miracle birth of your Son, even in less than ideal circumstances. Help us to truly honor you, no matter what the days ahead may bring. Amen.

THOUGHT TO PONDER

When Mary birthed Jesus
'Twas in a cow's stall,
With wise men and farmers
And shepherds and all.
But high from God's heaven
A star's light did fall,
And the promise of ages
It then did recall

-- *Appalachian carol, collected by John Jacob Niles, "I Wonder As I Wander," stanza 2*

DISCUSSION QUESTIONS FOR A SUNDAY MEAL

- What part of Christmas do you enjoy celebrating most?
- What circumstances are you facing this year that are less than ideal?
- How can you make certain you celebrate Jesus' birth anyway?
- Have you ever felt, once Christmas was over, that you had missed celebrating Christ's birthday? How can you make sure that doesn't happen this year?

For Individuals or Couples

This ceremony can be used the fourth Sunday of Advent by individuals or couples.

The Fourth Candle: Celebrate Whatever Your Circumstances.

Candle Lighting: As we light the fourth candle, the season of Advent is drawing to a close. Let this candle symbolize the truth that we can celebrate Christmas no matter what the circumstances we face.

New Testament Scripture: Read Luke 2:6-20

Reflection: The first Christmas was celebrated in a stable, difficult circumstances for the birth of a child. And yet the angels sang. The shepherds worshiped. Mary and Joseph delighted in the coming of God's newborn king.

Prayer: Father, Christmas is coming quickly, and still we long for the perfect celebration. Remind us again that we can joyously honor Christ's birth no matter what our personal circumstances. Your Son was born to the smell of the animals, and the scratch of the straw. Help us remember that whatever the days ahead may bring our way, we too can celebrate the miracle birth of our King. Amen.

Old Testament Scripture: Read Psalm 89:1-8

Sing: Sing a favorite hymn or Christmas carol.

For Families With Young Children

This ceremony can be used the fourth Sunday of Advent by families with young children.

The Fourth Candle: Celebrate Whatever Your Circumstances

Parent: Today we light the fourth candle in our Advent wreath

Children: Christmas is almost here!

Parent: Help us remember we can celebrate, even if things aren't perfect. We might be tired on Christmas. Or sick. Maybe we won't get all the presents we wanted. Maybe we won't get to see our favorite friends and relatives. We can still celebrate!

Children: Christmas is almost here!

Parent: Remember the first Christmas? It had some hard parts, too. There was no room in the inn for Mary and Joseph. Jesus was born in a stable. But still, they celebrated.

Children: Christmas is almost here!

Parent: As we light the fourth candle, let's promise to celebrate Christ's birth. Even if things aren't perfect. *[Light the fourth candle]*

All together: Christmas is almost here!

MONDAY
Advent Week 4

TODAY'S SCRIPTURE

And there were shepherds living out in the fields nearby, keeping watch over their flocks at night. An angel of the Lord appeared to them, and the glory of the Lord shone around them, and they were terrified. (Luke 2:8-9)

JOURNAL THOUGHTS

_____

_____

_____

_____

_____

_____

TODAY'S PRAYER

Lord, your angels announced Christ's birth to ordinary shepherds. Help us remember that we can celebrate Christmas no matter how ordinary or less than ideal our lives may be. Amen.

THOUGHT TO PONDER

He came down to earth from heaven,

Who is God and Lord of all,

And His shelter was a stable,

And His cradle was a stall;

With the poor, the scorned, the lowly,

Lived on earth our Savior holy.

-- Cecil F. Alexander, *"Once in Royal David's City,"* stanza 2

PRACTICAL SUGGESTIONS

For Families: Observe Travelers

Spend an evening at a nearby airport, train terminal, or bus station (or coordinate this with an already planned pick-up or send-off of a friend or relative). Get a bite to eat and then go people-watching. Talk to your children about how Joseph and Mary had to take a long, tiresome trip during the time she was expecting Jesus. Look for ways to minister to weary travelers. Give out small inexpensive toys or Christmas books to children while offering an empathetic smile to their parents.

For Individuals: Be Anonymous

Help someone celebrate by asking the Lord to put on your heart the name of a person who could use a little extra money at the last minute to make ends meet this Christmas. Maybe it's a single parent or an older person who comes to mind. Arrange to give your gift anonymously so that the recipient perceives this help as coming from the Lord.

Advent Week 1

TODAY'S SCRIPTURE

But the angel said to [the shepherds], "Do not be afraid. I bring you good news of great joy that will be for all the people. Today in the town of David a Savior has been born to you; he is Christ the Lord. (Luke 2:10-11)

JOURNAL THOUGHTS

\
\
\
\
\
\
\
\
\
\
\
\
\

TODAY'S PRAYER

Father, in our present circumstances let us experience great joy in celebrating the birth of our Savior. Amen.

THOUGHT TO PONDER

"There is no better place for me to become like Jesus than my present circumstances."
-- *Marie Chapian*

PRACTICAL SUGGESTIONS

For Families: Read the Christmas Story

Take 15 minutes to get together as a family and read the Christmas story (Luke 1:1-2:20). One person might read while others listen, or everyone could take turns.

For Individuals: Adjust Your Impulse

Check your impulse to focus on the negative during this hectic season, especially when circumstances seem less than ideal. Are you constantly rehearsing a litany of woes to your friends? Work instead at focusing on God's great promises. In public, make a choice to give testimony to God's continued goodness in spite of real and pressing problems. In private, thank God for every evidence of his care, both large and small, regardless of whether or not your major problems have been resolved.

Advent Week 4

TODAY'S SCRIPTURE

"This will be a sign to you: You will find a baby wrapped in cloths and lying in a manger" (Luke 2:12)

JOURNAL THOUGHTS

_____

_____

_____

_____

_____

_____

_____

_____

TODAY'S PRAYER

Father, let your son's birth be a sign to us, as it was to the shepherds, of your unfailing love. Help us to celebrate your great gift no matter what our circumstances this Christmas. Amen.

THOUGHT TO PONDER

There was a gift for each of us left under the tree of life 2,000 years ago by him whose birthday we celebrate today. The gift was withheld from no man. Some have left their package unclaimed. Some have accepted the gift and carry it around, but have failed to remove the wrappings and look inside to uncover the hidden splendour. The packages are all alike: in each is a scroll on which is written, "All that the Father hath is thine. Take and live!"

-- *First Baptist Church Bulletin, Syracuse, New York*

Practical Suggestions

For Families: Let Your Light Shine

Some Christmas traditions include placing lights in the windows of your home or apartment. Some people use oil-lit glass lanterns around the house only at Christmastime. In the southwestern United States, luminaria (paper bags with sand on the bottom to anchor a votive candle) line walks and driveways to light the way for the Christ child. As a family think about how to use light as a symbol of Christ's arrival this Christmas.

For Individuals: Go on a Christmas Search

Don't just gloss over all you've accomplished this Christmas season. Take some time to search for ways this has been the Christmas you've always longed for. And think back about God's role in the whole process. What has God done for you this Christmas season? What has God done through you for others this Christmas season?

Advent Week 4

TODAY'S SCRIPTURE

Suddenly a great company of the heavenly host appeared with the angel, praising God and saying, "Glory to God in the highest, and on earth peace to men on whom his favor rests" (Luke 2:13-14)

JOURNAL THOUGHTS

_____

_____

_____

_____

_____

_____

_____

_____

TODAY'S PRAYER

God, this Christmas lift our hearts in praise to you, and let us know your peace in our present circumstances. Amen.

THOUGHT TO PONDER

The universal joy of Christmas is certainly wonderful. We ring the bells when princes are born, or toll a mournful dirge when great men pass away. Nations have their red-letter days, their carnivals and festivals, but once in the year and only once, the whole world stands still to celebrate the advent of a life. Only Jesus of Nazareth claims this worldwide, undying remembrance. You cannot cut Christmas out of the calendar, nor out of the heart of the world.

-- Anonymous

PRACTICAL SUGGESTIONS

For Families: Hold a Christmas Award Night

Celebrate this year's Christmas by congratulating all in your family for a way in which they helped make this year's Christmas special. Make sure everyone gets an award. Consider awards for Most Relaxed, Best Time Manager, Most Supportive, and so on.

For Individuals: Reach Out

Is there someone you should "touch" by telephone this Christmas? Think of someone near or far who has experienced a painful loss this year, such as a business failure, a divorce, or a death in the family. Unfortunately, at Christmas many people avoid talking to those who are experiencing emotional pain because they think talking about the problem will "depress" them further. This is seldom the case. When you call, begin the conversation by saying, "I've been thinking about you this Christmas, and I just wanted to see how you're doing." Then let the other person take the lead.

Advent Week 4

TODAY'S SCRIPTURE

When the angels had left them and gone into heaven, the shepherds said to one another, "Let's go to Bethlehem and see this thing that has happened, which the Lord has told us about." So they hurried off and found Mary and Joseph, and the baby, who was lying in the manger. (Luke 2:15-16)

JOURNAL THOUGHTS

_____

_____

_____

_____

_____

_____

_____

TODAY'S PRAYER

Lord, we want to see afresh this miracle birth that happened in Bethlehem. Help us remember you and celebrate no matter what our present lives may be like. Amen.

THOUGHT TO PONDER

We rejoice in the light,

And we echo the song

That comes down through the night

From the heavenly throng.

Ay! we shout to the lovely evangel they bring,

And we greet in His cradle our Savior and King.

-- *Josiah Gilbert Holland, "A Christmas Carol"*

PRACTICAL SUGGESTIONS

For Families: Write the Christmas Times

If your family were writing newspaper articles about this year's Christmas experience, what would the headlines be? Let each family member come up with a headline of their own. You may even want to write the first sentence or two of the articles. Then read them to each other, or write them all down on a piece of paper or poster board.

For Individuals: Celebrate with Christ

If circumstances like weather, illness, or work have you alone on this year's holiday, don't forgo a celebration. Make a favorite dessert even if you can't possibly finish it, set the table with your good china, play Christmas music, enjoy a favorite book, or treat yourself to a long-distance phone call to a relative or old friend. Remember, you can't really be alone at a Christmas celebration. Christ is always with you, and it's his birthday you're celebrating.

Advent Week 4

TODAY'S SCRIPTURE

When they had seen him, they spread the word concerning what had been told them about this child, and all who heard it were amazed at what the shepherds said to them (Luke 2:17-18)

JOURNAL THOUGHTS

_____

_____

_____

_____

_____

_____

_____

_____

_____

_____

TODAY'S PRAYER

Father, even in less than ideal circumstances, help us celebrate by worshiping you and sharing your love with others. Amen.

THOUGHTS TO PONDER

Christmas is a time for "giving up" sin, bad habits, and selfish pleasures. Christmas is a time for "giving in" surrender to Christ, acceptance of him as King. Christmas is a time for "giving out" real giving, not swapping.

-- *Anonymous*

Practical Suggestions

For Families: Make a Birthday Cake Dessert

Consider making the dessert for your Christmas dinner a birthday cake for Jesus, complete with lighted candles (or put candles on the dessert you were already planning). The youngest family member present could blow out the candles after everyone has sung "Happy Birthday" to Jesus.

For Individuals: Give a Birthday Gift to Jesus

Have you ever thought of surprising Christ by giving him a gift for his birthday? A half hour set apart for quiet reflection upon the meaning of Christ's birth would be a most appropriate way to celebrate his coming.

HOME CEREMONY
Christmas Day

TODAY'S SCRIPTURE

But Mary treasured up all these things and pondered them in her heart. The shepherds returned, glorifying and praising God for all the things they had heard and seen, which were just as they had been told. (Luke 2:19-20)

JOURNAL THOUGHTS

_____

_____

_____

_____

_____

_____

_____

_____

TODAY'S PRAYER

Father although these days of Advent have been hectic, you know we have tried to please you with our worship. Thank you for the quiet serenity you have placed in our hearts and for reminding us that because of your Son we can enjoy the Christmas we've always longed for. Amen.

THOUGHT TO PONDER

I do hope your Christmas has had a little touch of Eternity in among the rush and pitter patter and all. It always seems such a mixing of this world and the next—but that after all is the idea!

-- Evelyn Underhill, *The Letters of Evelyn Underhill, Christmas Day, 1936*

For Families, Couples, and Individuals

The Fifth Candle: Enjoy a God-pleasing Christmas.

Candle Lighting: The fifth and final candle in the Advent wreath is sometimes called the Christ candle. The lighting of the Christ candle marks the conclusion of our time of waiting and preparation. It signifies the birth of Christ in Bethlehem: the heart of the Christmas celebration.

New Testament Scripture: Read Luke 1:26-33; 2:1-20.

Reflection: Mary, Christ's mother, obeyed God in all he asked, then watched him unfold the Christmas miracle. In the same way she "treasured up" all the events surrounding that first Christmas and "pondered them in her heart," we too can embrace and enjoy the wonder of a God-pleasing Christmas.

Prayer: Father, thank you for the gift of Jesus Christ. Throughout this season of Advent our desire has been to please you and to place Christ at the center of all we have done. Today and in the days ahead, help us to treasure up and ponder the greatest gift of all—your Son—as we enjoy a Christmas celebration that is pleasing to you. Amen.

Old Testament Scripture: Read Isaiah 40:9-11

Sing: "Joy to the World"

Notes

Notes

Preparing for Next Year's Nativity Season

Most women who are pregnant either purchase or are given a birthing manual. One highly popular pregnancy guide is titled What to Expect When You're Expecting. In a comprehensive month-by-month format, it assists the mother-to-be in knowing exactly what she can expect to happen. The last chapter, "Preparing for the Next Baby," includes 24 specific suggestions.

Since preparation for physical birth can be a metaphor for preparing for spiritual birth and growth, some of the suggestions apply directly to getting ready for next year's Christmas season. The authors suggest anyone wanting to prepare for the next birth should get a thorough physical, select a practitioner (and have a pre-pregnancy exam), correct any health problems, start keeping track, and eliminate any toxins in their system.

In a similar way, you can prepare yourself to create the next "Christmas you've always longed for." You can:

Get a Thorough Physical. Examine this Christmas and diagnose what was good and what was not so good. This will not only help you with Christmas preparation but will establish healthy principles for many areas of your life.

Select a Practitioner. We all need models and mentors. Did you notice any Christians who seem to have discovered the secret to observing holy festivals? Set a time to talk to them about how they've learned to do this.

Correct Your Essential Health Problems. Intriguingly, this process begins by assessing our own inner attitudes. What have you discovered about yourself this Christmas that can help you create a better Christmas next year?

Start Keeping Track. You are looking toward the rest of a lifetime of Christmas celebrations. Improvement doesn't stop after one year. Start a journal or begin a "Christmas" folder.

Rid Yourself of Toxins. Less is always more. Discard all the too-much areas in your life. What did you not need this year? Are there Christmas incidents you should forgive? People to whom you should apologize? Detoxify all the negatives from this year now, so they don't keep you from making next year "the Christmas you've always longed for."